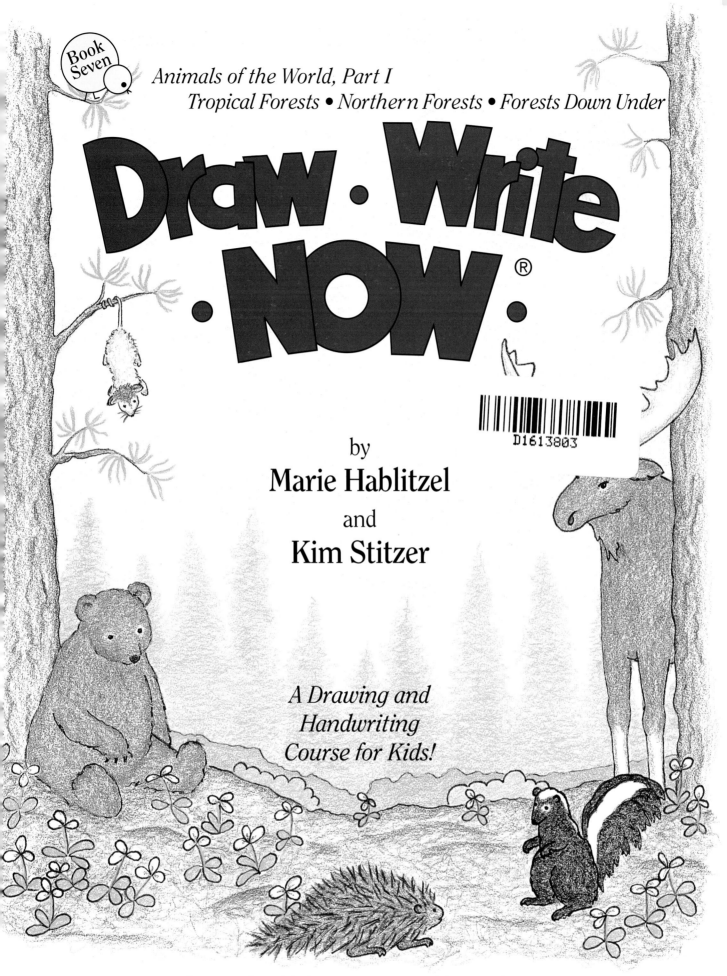

Book Seven

Animals of the World, Part I
Tropical Forests • Northern Forests • Forests Down Under

Draw · Write · NOW ®

by
Marie Hablitzel
and
Kim Stitzer

D1613803

A Drawing and
Handwriting
Course for Kids!

Barker Creek Publishing, Inc. • Poulsbo, Washington

Dedicated to...

...my grandchildren.
I have enjoyed drawing with you! — M.H.

...Carolyn Hurst — K.S.

The text on the handwriting pages is set in a custom
font created from Marie Hablitzel's handwriting.
The drawings are done using Prismacolor pencils
outlined with a black PaperMate FLAIR!® felt tip pen.

BARKER CREEK
Published by Barker Creek Publishing, Inc.
P.O. Box 2610 • Poulsbo, WA 98370-2610
800•692•5833 FAX: 360•613•2542
www.barkercreek.com

Text and Illustration Copyright © 2000 by Kim Hablitzel Stitzer

Book layout by Judy Richardson
Printed in Hong Kong

Library of Congress Catalog Card Number: 93-73893

Publisher's Cataloging in Publication Data:
Hablitzel, Marie, 1920 -
Draw•Write•Now®, Book Seven: A drawing and handwriting course for kids!
(seventh in series)
Summary: A collection of drawing and handwriting lessons for children. **Book Seven** focuses on Forest Animals of the World: Tropical Forests, Northern Forests, Forests Down Under. Seventh book in the ***Draw•Write•Now®*** series. — 1st ed.
1. Drawing — Technique — Juvenile Literature. 2. Drawing — Study and Teaching (Elementary). 3. Penmanship. 4. Forest Animals — Juvenile Literature. 5. Cartography — Juvenile Literature. 6. Map Drawing — Juvenile Literature. 7. Animals — Juvenile Literature. 8. Australia — Juvenile Literature.
I. Stitzer, Kim, 1956 -   , coauthor. II. Title.
741.2   [372.6] — dc 19

ISBN: 0-9639307-7-X

Sixth Printing

About this book...

For most children, drawing is their first form of written communication. Long before they master the alphabet and sentence syntax, children express themselves creatively on paper through line and color.

As children mature, their imaginations often race ahead of their drawing skills. By teaching them to see complex objects as combinations of simple shapes and encouraging them to develop their fine-motor skills through regular practice, they can better record the images they see so clearly in their minds.

This book contains a collection of beginning drawing lessons and text for practicing handwriting. These lessons were developed by a teacher who saw her second-grade students becoming increasingly frustrated with their drawing efforts and disenchanted with repetitive handwriting drills.

For more than 30 years, Marie Hablitzel refined what eventually became a daily drawing and handwriting curriculum. Marie's premise was simple — drawing and handwriting require many of the same skills. And, regular practice in a supportive environment is the key to helping children develop

Coauthors Marie Hablitzel (left)
and her daughter, Kim Stitzer

their technical skills, self-confidence and creativity. As a classroom teacher, Marie intertwined her daily drawing and handwriting lessons with math, science, social studies, geography, reading and creative writing. She wove an educational tapestry that hundreds of children have found challenging, motivating — and fun!

Although Marie is now retired, her drawing and handwriting lessons continue to be used in the classroom. With the assistance of her daughter, Kim Stitzer, Marie shares more than 150 of her lessons in the eight-volume *Draw•Write•Now*® series.

In *Draw•Write•Now*®, *Book One*, children explore life on a farm, kids and critters and storybook characters. *Books Two* through *Six* feature topics as diverse as Christopher Columbus, the weather, Native Americans, the polar regions, young Abraham Lincoln, beaver ponds and life in the sea. In *Draw•Write•Now*®, *Books Seven and Eight*, children circle the globe while learning about animals of the world.

We hope your children and students enjoy these lessons as much as ours have!

— *Carolyn Hurst, Publisher*

Look for these books
in the *Draw•Write•Now,*® series...

Book One: On the Farm, Kids and Critters, Storybook Characters
Book Two: Christopher Columbus, Autumn Harvest, The Weather
Book Three: Native Americans, North America, The Pilgrims
Book Four: The Polar Regions, The Arctic, The Antarctic
Book Five: The United States, From Sea to Sea, Moving Forward
Book Six: Animals & Habitats: On Land, Ponds and Rivers, Oceans
Book Seven: Animals of the World, Part I: Forest Animals
Book Eight: Animals of the World, Part II: Grassland and Desert Animals

For additional information call 1-800-692-5833
or visit barkercreek.com

Table of Contents

A table of contents is like a map. It guides you to the places you want to visit in a book. Pick a subject you want to draw, then turn to the page listed beside the picture.

For more information on the *Draw•Write•Now*® series, see page 3. For suggestions on how to use this book, see page 6.

Animals of the Tropical Forests Page 9

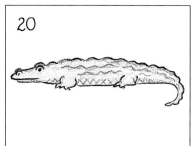

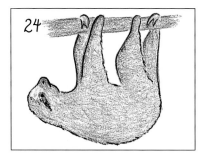
Animals of the Northern Forests Page 29

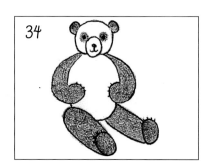

Forest Animals Down Under

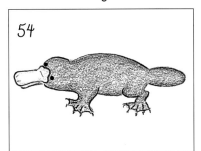

Teaching Tips

A few tips to get started...

This is a book for children and their parents, teachers and caregivers. Although most young people can complete the lessons in this book quite successfully on their own, a little help and encouragement from a caring adult can go a long way toward building a child's self-confidence, creativity and technical skills.

Koala by Claire Cardoso, age 8
from Draw•Write•Now®, Book Seven

The following outline contains insights from the 30-plus years the authors have worked with the material in this book. Realizing that no two children or classrooms are alike, the authors encourage you to modify these lessons to best suit the needs of your child or classroom. Each *Draw•Write•Now®* lesson includes five parts:

1. Introduce the subject.
2. Draw the subject.
3. Draw the background.
4. Practice handwriting.
5. Color the drawing.

Each child will need a pencil, an eraser, drawing paper, penmanship paper and either crayons, color pencils or felt tip markers to complete each lesson as presented here.

1. Introduce the Subject

Begin the lesson by generating interest in the subject with a story, discussion, poem, photograph or song. The questions on the illustrated notes scattered throughout this book are examples of how interest can be built along a related theme. Answers to these questions and the titles of several theme-related books are on pages 28, 50 and 62.

2. Draw the Subject

Have the children draw with a pencil. Encourage them to draw lightly because some lines (shown as dashed lines on the drawing lessons) will need to be erased. Point out the shapes and lines in the subject as the children work through the lesson. Help the children see that complex objects can be viewed as combinations of lines and simple shapes.

Help the children be successful! Show them how to position the first step on their papers in an appropriate size. Initially, the children may find some shapes difficult to draw. If they do, provide a pattern for them to trace, or draw the first step for them. Once they fine-tune their skills and build their self-confidence, their ability and creativity will take over. For lesson-specific drawing tips and suggestions, refer to *Teaching Tips* on pages 63–64.

3. Draw the Background

Encourage the children to express their creativity and imaginations in the backgrounds they add to their pictures. Add to their creative libraries by demonstrating various ways to draw trees, horizons and other details. Point out background details in the drawings in this book, illustrations from other books, photographs and works of art.

Encourage the children to draw their world by looking for basic shapes and lines in the things they see around them. Ask them to draw from their imaginations by using their developing skills. For additional ideas on motivating children to draw creatively, see pages 26–27, 48–49 and 60–61.

4. Practice Handwriting

In place of drills — rows of e's, r's and so on — it is often useful and more motivating to have children write complete sentences when they practice their handwriting. When the focus is on handwriting rather than spelling or vocabulary enrichment, use simple words that the children can easily read and spell. Begin by writing each sentence with the children, demonstrating how individual letters are formed and stressing proper spacing. Start slowly. One or two sentences may be challenging enough in the beginning. Once the children are consistently forming their letters correctly, encourage them to work at their own pace.

There are many ways to adapt these lessons for use with your child or classroom. For example, you may want to replace the authors' text with your own words. You may want to let the children compose sentences to describe their drawings or answer the theme-related questions found throughout the book. You may prefer to replace the block alphabet used in this book with a cursive, D'Nealian® or other alphabet style. If you are unfamiliar with the various alphabet styles used for teaching handwriting, consult your local library. A local elementary school may also be able to recommend an appropriate alphabet style and related resource materials.

5. Color the Picture

Children enjoy coloring their own drawings. The beautiful colors, however, often cover the details they have so carefully drawn in pencil. To preserve their efforts, you may want to have the children trace their pencil lines with black crayons or fine-tipped felt markers.

Crayons — When they color with crayons, have the children outline their drawings with a black crayon *after* they have colored their pictures (the black crayon may smear if they do their outlining first).

Statue of Liberty by Anne Morrison, age 8
from Draw•Write•Now®, Book Five

Pig by Lia Huking, age 6
from Draw•Write•Now®, Book One

Color Pencils — When they color with color pencils, have the children outline their drawings with a felt tip marker *before* they color their drawings.

Felt Tip Markers — When they color with felt tip markers, have the children outline their drawings with a black marker *after* they have colored their pictures.

Your comments are appreciated!
How are you sharing Draw•Write•Now® with your children or students? The authors would appreciate hearing from you. Write to Marie Hablitzel and Kim Stitzer, c/o Barker Creek Publishing, Inc., P.O. Box 2610, Poulsbo, WA 98370, USA or visit us at barkercreek.com.

Dogs with Rabbit by Cameron Adams, age 7
from Draw•Write•Now®, Book One

Handwriting is an Art!

Practice Handwriting Carefully

1. Sit up straight.
2. Hold your pencil correctly.
3. Use the paper guidelines.
4. Form each letter carefully.
5. Space the words evenly.
6. Practice daily.

The more you practice, the better your writing will look!

Forest Animals of the Tropics

Living in the Tropical Forests of the World

Asian elephants live in Asia. Another species of elephant lives in Africa.

Asian elephants are huge.

They have tough skin.

Some Asian elephants work.

People use them to carry things.

What can an elephant do with its trunk?

Elephant

Question answered on page 28

Asian Elephant

1.

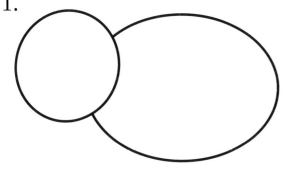

2.

3.

4.

5.

6.

Tiger

Question answered on page 28
Teaching Tip on page 64

Bengal Tiger

1.

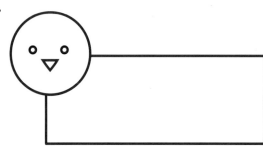

2.

3.

4.

5.

6.

Tigers live in Asia. Bengal tigers live in southern Asia.

Tigers are the largest cats.
They are very powerful.
Tigers hunt in tall grass.
Their stripes help them hide.

Where can you find
lions, tigers and
bears? (Oh my!)

Chimpanzees live in Africa.

Chimpanzees climb trees.

Their hands and feet grip well.

Chimpanzees perch on branches.

Trees are good resting places.

Are chimpanzees monkeys?

1.

2.

3.

4.

5.

6.

7.

8.

9.

10.

Leopard

Question answered on page 28
Teaching Tip on page 64

1.

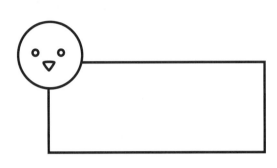

2.

3.

4.

5.

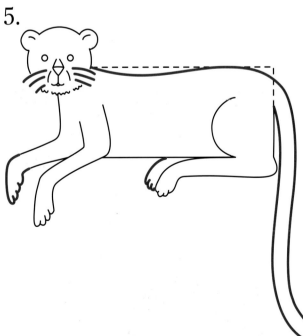

6.

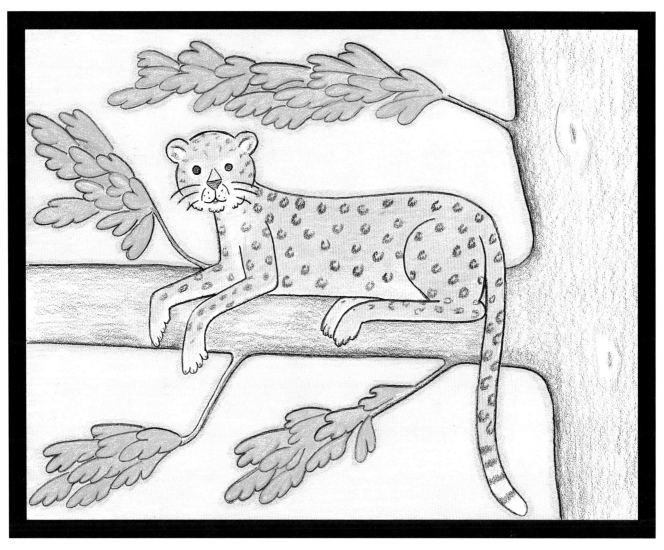

Leopards live in Asia and Africa.

Leopards are strong cats.
They drag their food up trees.
Leopards rest on the branches.
Their spots help them hide.

Female Lion
(no pattern)

How does spotted fur help leopards hide?

Leopard
(spots)

Tiger
(stripes)

Spider monkeys live in South America. Other types of monkeys live in South America, Africa and Asia.

The world has many monkeys.
Each is different.
Spider monkeys are lively.
They hang from their tails.

Can all monkeys hang from their tails?

Monkey

Question answered on page 28
Teaching Tip on page 64

Spider Monkey

1.

2.

3.

4.

5.

6.

7.

8.

9.

1.

2.

3.

4.

Alligator

Question answered on page 28

North American Alligator

1.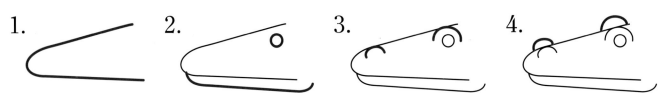

2.

3.

4.

5.

6.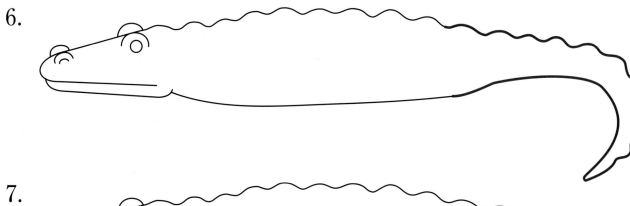

7.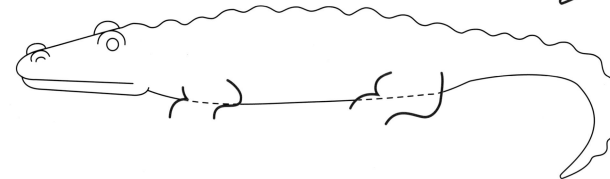

8.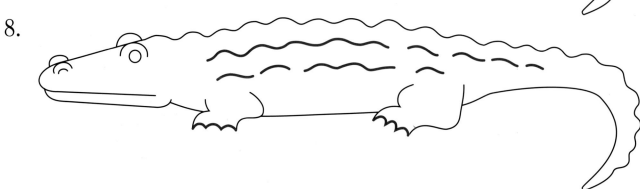

North American alligators live in North America. Other species of alligators live in South America.

Alligators crawl on land.

Their babies hatch from eggs.

Alligators swim in water.

Water helps them hide.

How big do alligators grow?

Toucans live in South America.

Toucans fly through the forest.
They are easy to see.
They flap and glide.

Is the toucan's beak heavy?

They are brightly colored.

Question answered on page 28

1.

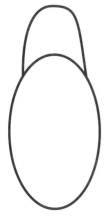

2.

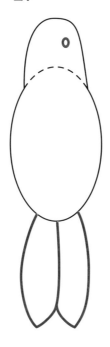

3.

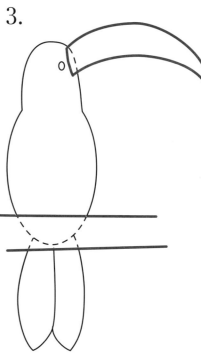

4.

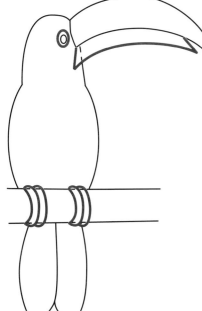

5.

6.

Sloth

Question answered on page 28
Teaching Tip on page 64

Two-Toed Sloth

1.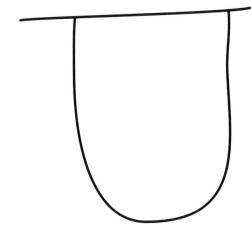

2.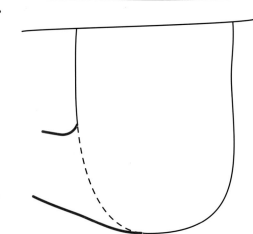

3.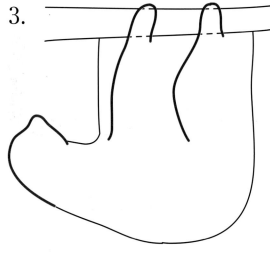

4.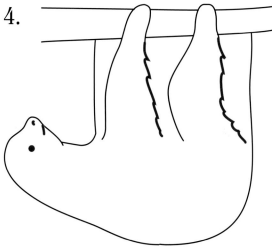

5.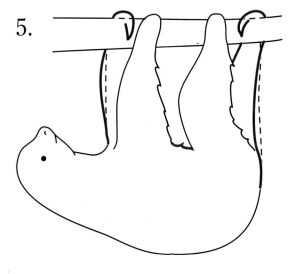

6.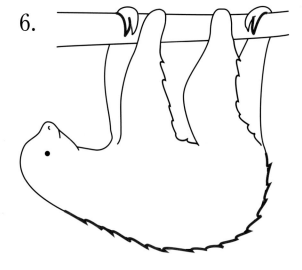

Sloths live in South America.

The sloth moves very slowly.
One arm shifts on the branch.
Another arm carefully follows.
A sloth even eats slowly!

Do sloths walk on the ground?

Draw From Your Imagination

Mapmakers help us identify places on Earth.
They start with a model of the earth — a globe.

Learn about animals and see where they live.

A dot or short line marks the North Pole. . .

and the South Pole.

A line drawn between the poles marks the Prime Meridian.

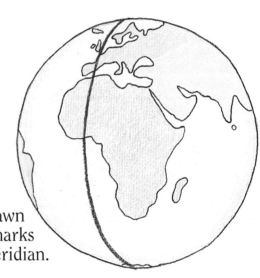

Which is easier to put in your pocket, a globe or a flat map?

A line drawn around the middle of the world marks the Equator.

Question answered on page 62

Draw a globe.

1. Mark the North Pole and the South Pole

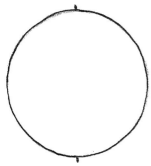

2. Draw the Prime Meridian

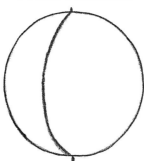

3. Draw the Equator

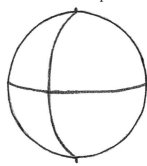

4. Draw and color the land.

5. Draw and color more land.

6. Color the oceans

Mapmakers can create another kind of model — a flat map. Can you name the mapmaking lines used on a flat map?

Fold a piece of paper in half

Fold it in half again

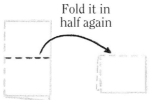

Unfold the paper

1.

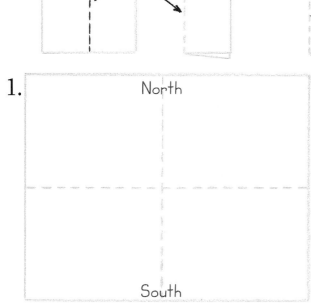

North

South

2.

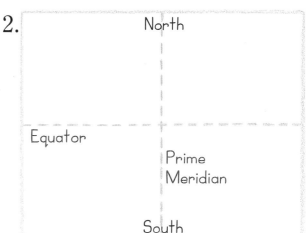

North

Equator

Prime Meridian

South

Learn more about tropical forest animals...

WHAT CAN AN ELEPHANT DO WITH ITS TRUNK?   PAGE 10

An elephant's trunk is like a nose and hand combined. It can sniff, lift a heavy log, or pick a blade of grass. See a clever little elephant in hot, hot India cool his mother, a rhinoceros and a tiger in SPLASH! *written and illustrated by Flora McDonnell, published by Candlewick Press, 1999. Then see how working elephants and wild elephants live in Asia with* IN THE VILLAGE OF THE ELEPHANTS *by Jeremy Schmidt, photographed by Ted Wood, published by Walker, 1994.*

WHERE CAN YOU FIND LIONS, TIGERS AND BEARS? (OH MY!)   Page 13

Zoos, circuses and game farms are the only places in the world where lions, tigers and bears live in the same environment. Travel to India to the natural habitat of the Bengal tiger with HEART OF A TIGER *by Marsha Diane Arnold, illustrated by Jamichael Henterly, published by Dial, 1995. Then go to a zoo with* MY VISIT TO THE ZOO *written and illustrated by Aliki Brandenberg, published by HarperCollins, 1997.*

ARE CHIMPANZEES MONKEYS?   Page 14

No, chimpanzees are apes. Learn about apes — chimps, gibbons, orangutans and gorillas — with APES *by Tess Lemmon, illustrated by John Butler, published by Ticknor & Fields, 1993. What is an easy way to tell monkeys and apes apart? Most monkeys have tails — apes do not have tails.*

HOW DOES SPOTTED FUR HELP LEOPARDS HIDE?   Page 17

The leopards' beautiful fur camouflages the animals because the pattern of the fur mimics the light and dark patterns of the vegetation that surrounds them. In forests, patterned objects are harder to see than solid-colored objects. See photographs of the big cats in NATIONAL GEOGRAPHIC BOOK OF MAMMALS *published by The National Geographic Society, 1998. Compare the similarities of the leopard and the jaguar, a spotted cat native to South America, with* JAGUAR IN THE RAIN FOREST *by Joanne Ryder, illustrated by Michael Rothman, published by Morrow Junior, 1996.*

CAN ALL MONKEYS HANG FROM THEIR TAILS?   Page 18

No, only the monkeys living in the tall rainforest trees of South America can grab branches with their tails. See them swing in SO SAY THE LITTLE MONKEYS *by Nancy Van Laan, illustrated by Yumi Heo, published by Atheneum, 1998. Whether hanging from their tails or their arms, monkeys are a common sight in tropical villages and cities. Visit a village in India with* IN THE HEART OF THE VILLAGE *written and illustrated by Barbara Bash, published by Little Brown & Co., 1996. Visit a village in Africa with* LAKE OF THE BIG SNAKE *by Isaac Olaleye, illustrated by Claudia Shepard, published by Boyds Mill Press, 1998. Then visit South America with* THE SHAMAN'S APPRENTICE *by Lynne Cherry, illustrated by Mark Plotkin, published by Gulliver Books, 1998.*

HOW BIG DO ALLIGATORS GROW?   Page 21

Male alligators grow to be approximately 11 feet long — the length of a large car! See KEEPER OF THE SWAMP *by Ann Garrett, illustrated by Karen Chandler, published by Turtle Books, 1999.*

IS THE TOUCAN'S BEAK HEAVY?   Page 22

The toucan's beak may appear heavy and awkward, but it is light and useful for reaching small berries on long limbs. How does the toucan sleep? It simply turns its head and rests its beak on its back! Which beak is best: long, short, big or small? Meet the Australian birds who test that question in THE BEST BEAK IN BOONAROO BAY *written and illustrated by Narelle Oliver, published by Fulcrum, 1995.*

DO SLOTHS WALK ON THE GROUND?   Page 25

No, the sloth's curved claws — perfect for grabbing limbs — make walking and standing difficult. How do sloths get water to drink? Sloths get all the moisture they need from tree leaves. Visit their home in WELCOME TO THE GREENHOUSE *by Jane Yolen, illustrated by Laura Regan, published by Putnam, 1993.*

Animals of the Northern Forests

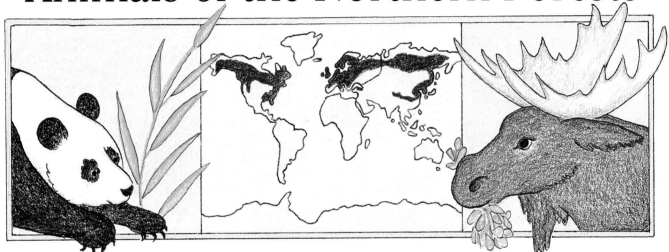

Living in the Northern Temperate Forests of the World

Grizzly bears live in North America. They are one of the brown bears of North America, Europe and Asia.

Grizzly bears are big.
Adults can be eight feet tall.
Grizzly bears are strong.
They can run fast.

What is a baby bear called?

Grizzly Bear

Question answered on page 50

1.

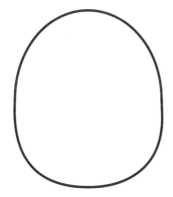

2.

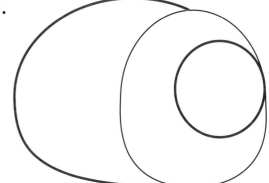

3.

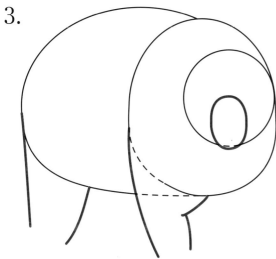

4.

5.

6.

Raccoon

Question answered on page 50

North American Raccoon

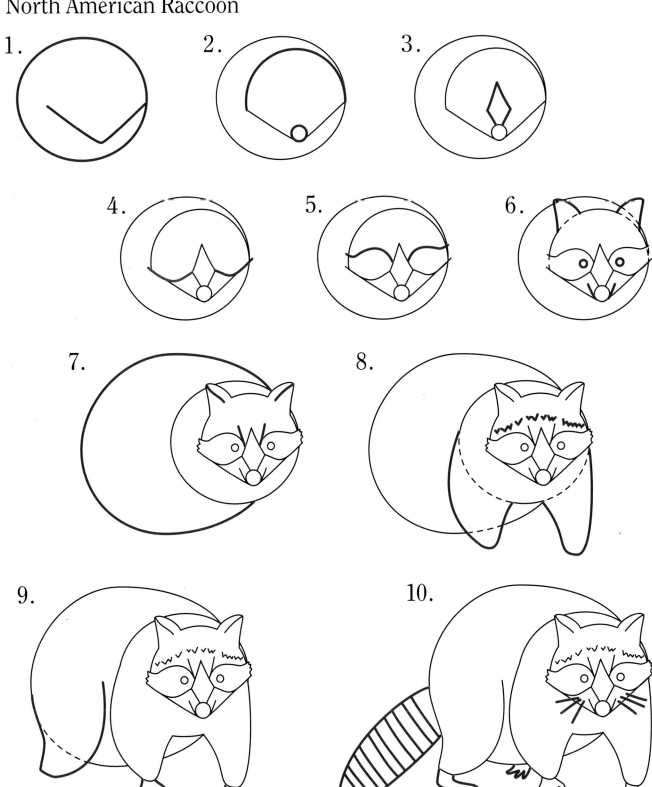

1.

2.

3.

4.

5.

6.

7.

8.

9.

10.

North American raccoons live in North America. Other species of raccoons live in South America.

Raccoons live in many places.
They like to be near water.
Their front paws are useful.
They can pick up objects.

Who is "The Bandit"?

33

Giant pandas live in Asia.

Pandas live in the mountains.
The weather is moist and cool.
Bamboo grows in the mountains.
Pandas eat bamboo.

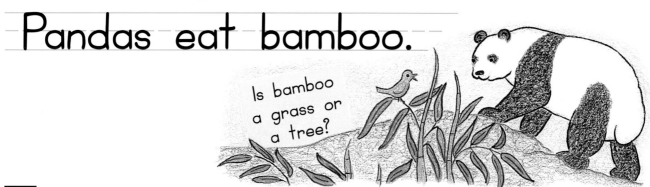

Is bamboo a grass or a tree?

1.

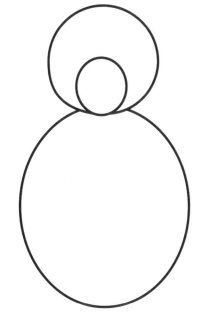

2.

3.

4.

Red Fox

Question answered on page 50
Teaching Tip on page 64

1.

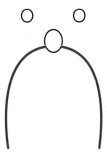

2.

3.

4.

5.

6.

7.

Red foxes live in North America, Europe, Asia and northern Africa.

The red fox can run fast.

It is difficult to chase.

The red fox is clever.

It can outsmart other animals.

How does the red fox trick other animals?

Little brown bats live in North America. Bats live everywhere except Antarctica and parts of the Arctic.

A bat flies in the dark.

It finds things with its ears.

The bat makes a sound.

It listens for the echo.

Can people hear the sounds bats make?

Little Brown Bat

Question answered on page 50

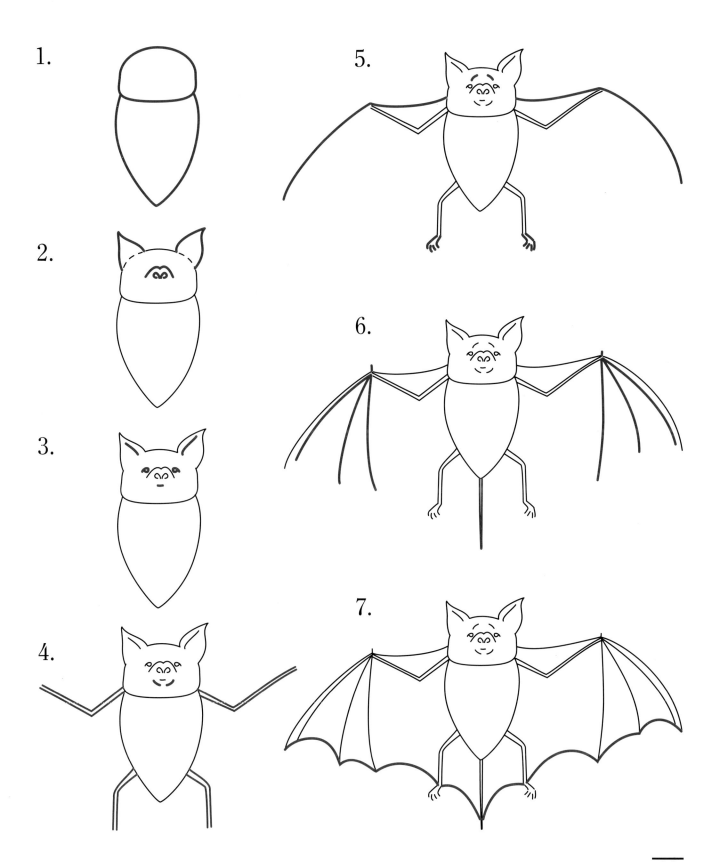

1.
2.
3.
4.
5.
6.
7.

Porcupine

Question answered on page 50
Teaching Tip on page 64

North American Porcupine

1.

2.

3.

4.

5.

6.

7.

8.

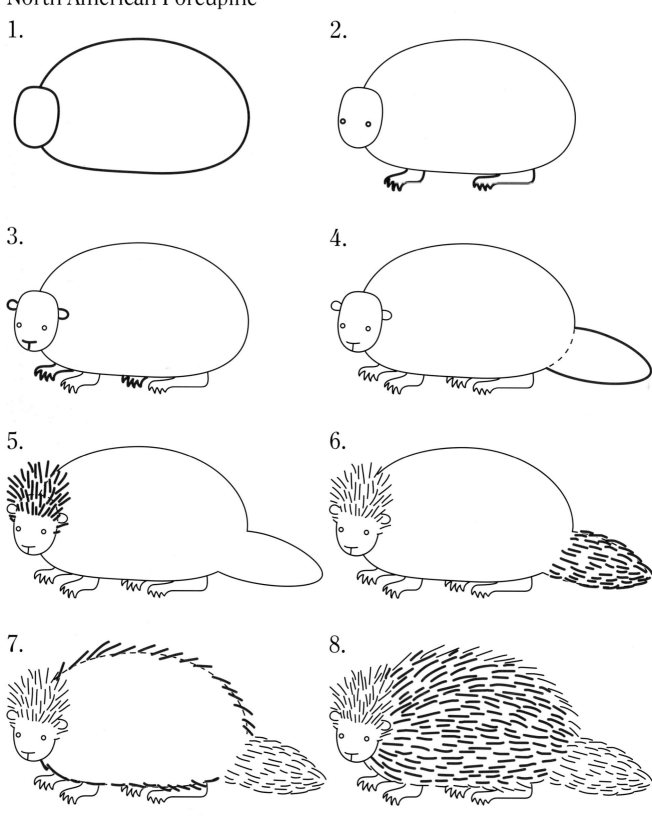

North American porcupines live in North America. Other species live in Europe, Africa and Asia.

Porcupines have sharp quills.
They keep porcupines safe.
The quills stick into enemies.
Quills hook into the skin.

Why are porcupine quills hard to remove?

Moose live in North America, Europe and Asia.

The moose has long legs.

Its neck is short.

Some plants are small.

A moose must kneel to eat.

Can moose swim?

Moose

Question answered on page 50

1.

2.

3.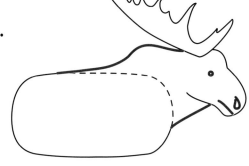

4.

5.

6.

Opossum

Question answered on page 50
Teaching Tip on page 64

Virginia Opossum

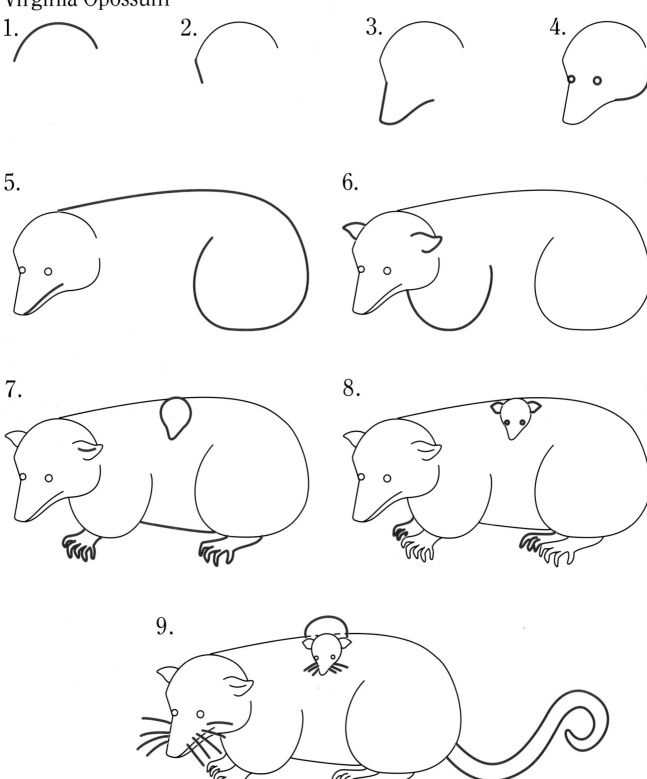

1.
2.
3.
4.
5.
6.
7.
8.
9.

Virginia opossums live in North America. Other opossum species live in South America.

A mother opossum has a pouch.

It is like a pocket.

Young babies stay safe inside.

Older babies cling to her back.

What does "playing 'possum" mean?

Striped skunks live in North America. Other species live in South America.

A skunk has a smelly liquid.
It is in bags near its tail.
A skunk lifts its tail to spray.
The smell is terrible!

Why do skunks spray?

Question answered on page 50

Striped Skunk

1.
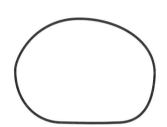

2.
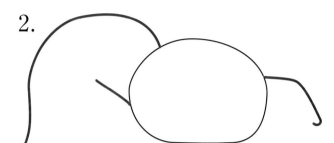

3.
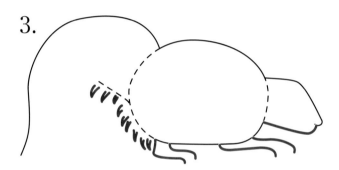

4.

5.

6.

7.

Draw Your World

Many animals on Earth live on the land. The seven large areas of land are called continents.

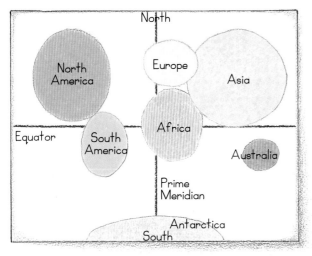

A simple map shows the location of each continent.

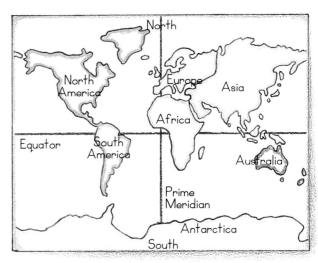

A detailed map shows the shape of each continent.

Compare a simple map to a detailed map.

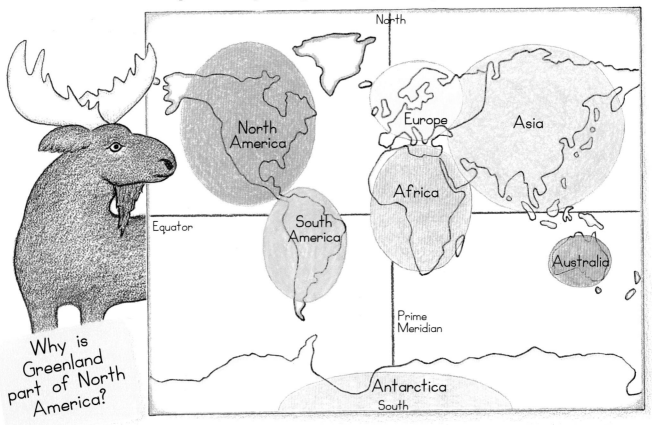

Why is Greenland part of North America?

(Greenland, the large island between North America and Europe, is outlined in orange on this map.) Question answered on page 62

Draw a simple map of the continents.

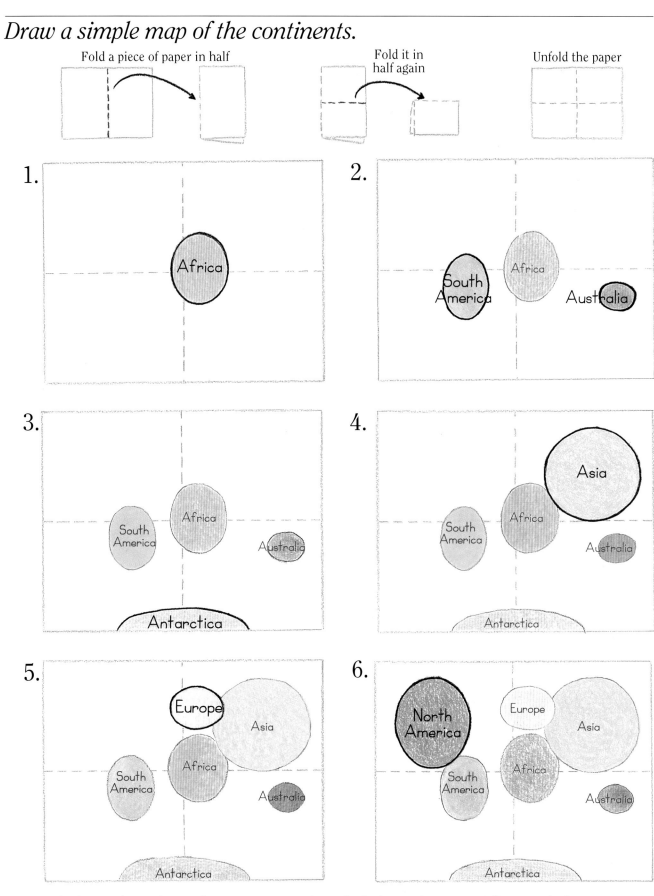

Fold a piece of paper in half

Fold it in half again

Unfold the paper

1.

2.

Africa

South America

Africa

Australia

3.

South America

Africa

Australia

Antarctica

4.

South America

Africa

Asia

Australia

Antarctica

5.

Europe

Asia

South America

Africa

Australia

Antarctica

6.

North America

Europe

Asia

South America

Africa

Australia

Antarctica

1. Label north and south on your map.

2. Label the Prime Meridian and the Equator.

Learn more about northern forest animals...

WHAT IS A BABY BEAR CALLED? Page 30

Baby bears are called cubs. Follow the life of a mother grizzly as she teaches her cub to hunt, play and find shelter in HONEY PAW AND LIGHTFOOT by Jonathan London, illustrated by Jon Van Zyle, published by Chronicle, 1995. Learn about bears in ALASKA'S THREE BEARS by Shannon Cartwright, illustrated by Shelley Gill, published by Sasquatch, 1990.

WHO IS "THE BANDIT"? Page 33

Raccoons, with their mask-like face markings and ability to get into people's possessions and garbage, have gained the reputation of being thieves! Understand why some wild animals choose to live near humans with WILD IN THE CITY written and illustrated by Jan Thornhill, published by Sierra Club Books, 1995. Then, see the animals in their natural environment with NORTH COUNTRY NIGHT written and illustrated by Daniel San Souci, published by Doubleday, 1990.

IS BAMBOO A GRASS OR A TREE? Page 34

Bamboo is a tall, heavy grass. Understand why bamboo is important to pandas' survival with BAMBOO VALLEY by Ann Whitehead Nagda, illustrated by Jim Effler, published by Soundprints, 1997.

HOW DOES THE RED FOX TRICK OTHER ANIMALS? Page 37

When chased, a red fox runs fast to get ahead then doubles back on its own trail and hides. The other animal runs past the hidden fox and continues to run in the direction of the fox's original path. By the time the animal realizes the fox is no longer running, the fox's trail and scent are lost. See WILD FOX by Cherie Mason, illustrated by JoEllen McAllister, published by Down East Books, 1993.

CAN PEOPLE HEAR THE SOUNDS BATS MAKE? Page 38

No, the sounds bats make — called echolocation — are at a frequency the human ear does not pick up. Learn about bats with SHADOWS OF NIGHT written and illustrated by Barbara Bash, published by Sierra Club Books, 1993. Hear the true story of a family who finds an orphaned baby bat in their house, then witnesses the return of its mother in THE BAT IN THE BOOT written and illustrated by Annie Cannon, published by Orchard, 1996.

WHY ARE PORCUPINE QUILLS HARD TO REMOVE? Page 41

The North American porcupine has barbed quills — quills with stiff scales on the tips which hook into the skin like a fishhook. Understand how painful and difficult these quills are to remove with BEN AND THE PORCUPINE by Carol Carrick, illustrated by Donald Carrick, published by Clarion, 1981.

CAN MOOSE SWIM? Page 42

Yes, moose can swim. Surprisingly, moose can dive 15 feet under water. Follow the life of a moose and calf in NORTHERN REFUGE by Audrey Fraggalosch, illustrated by Crista Forest, published by Soundprints, 1999. Then visit the Olympic National Forest and meet another large member of the deer family, the Roosevelt elk, in A NORTH AMERICAN RAIN FOREST SCRAPBOOK written and illustrated by Virginia Wright-Frierson, published by Walker, 1999.

WHAT DOES "PLAYING 'POSSUM" MEAN? Page 45

"Playing 'possum" means lying very still, as if asleep. It became a saying as people observed the opossum's unusual defense mechanism of lying motionless when threatened by another animal. Read OPOSSUM AT SYCAMORE ROAD by Sally M. Walker, illustrated by Joel Snyder, published by Soundprints, 1997.

WHY DO SKUNKS SPRAY? Page 46

Defense! Skunks give other animals plenty of opportunity to retreat but will spray if the animals continue to threaten them. See SKUNK AT HEMLOCK CIRCLE by Sally M. Walker, illustrated by Joel Snyder, published by Soundprints, 1997.

Forest Animals Down Under

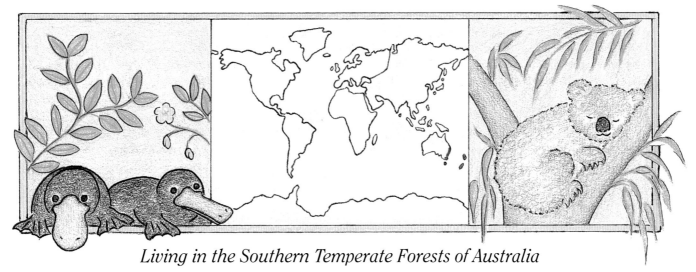

Living in the Southern Temperate Forests of Australia

Kangaroos live in Australia. Gray kangaroos live in the forests.

Mother kangaroo has a pouch.

It holds her baby.

The baby can climb in and out.

The baby is called a joey.

How far can a kangaroo jump?

Kangaroo

Question answered on page 62

Gray Kangaroo

1.
2.
3.
4.
5.
6.
7.
8.
9.
10.

Platypus

Question answered on page 62

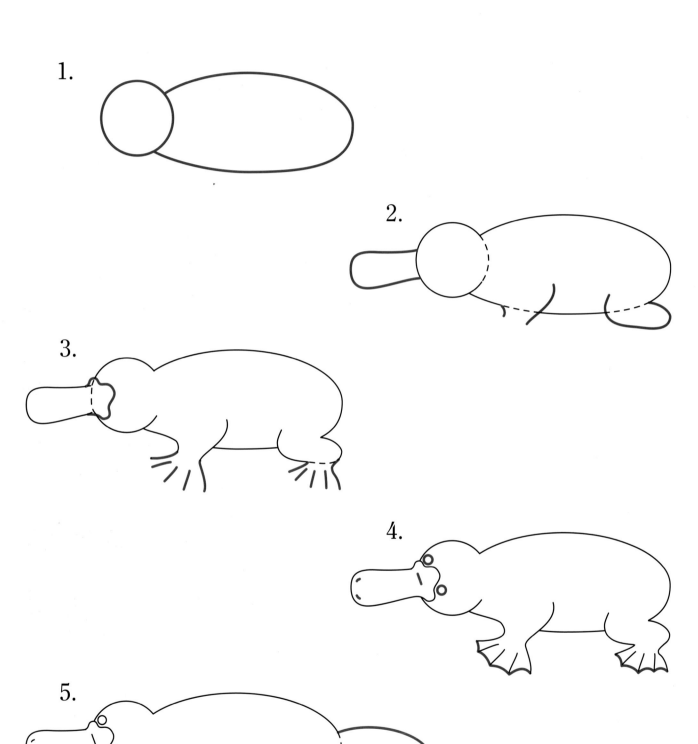

1.

2.

3.

4.

5.

Platypuses live in Australia near lakes, rivers and streams.

The platypus has a funny body.

It has a bill like a duck.

Its feet are webbed.

Its tail is flat.

Do platypuses quack?

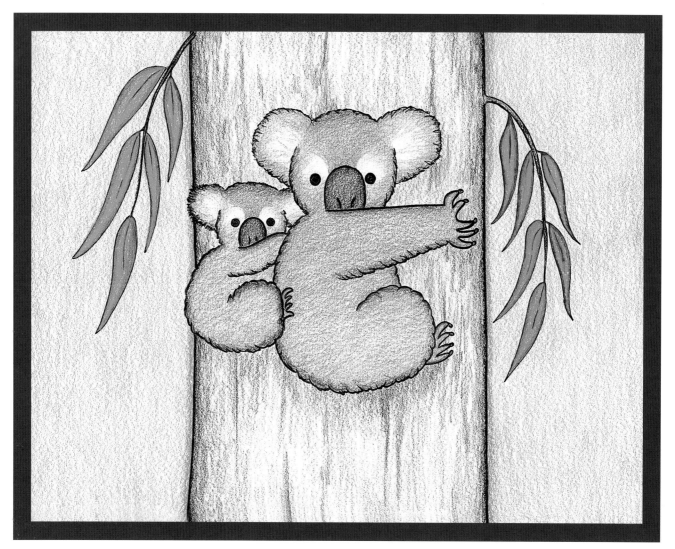

Koalas live in Australia in gum (eucalyptus) tree forests.

Koalas live in gum trees.

The leaves are their food.

The branches are their beds.

Koalas are safe in the trees.

Are koalas safe when they go for a drink of water?

Koala

Question answered on page 62
Teaching Tip on page 64

1.

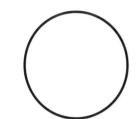

2.

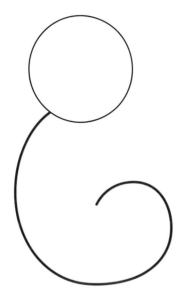

3.

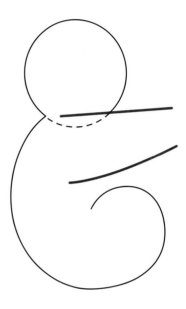

4.

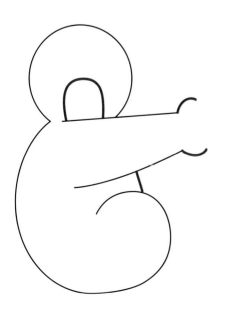

5.

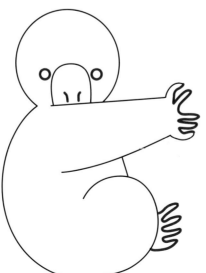

6.

Echidna

Question answered on page 62
Teaching Tip on page 64

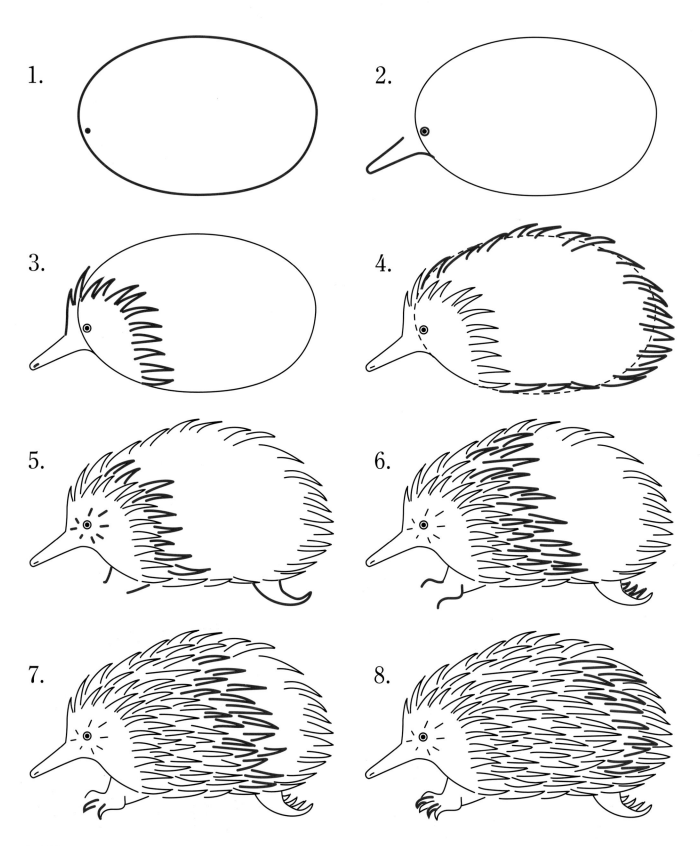

1.

2.

3.

4.

5.

6.

7.

8.

Echidnas live in Australia in forests, grasslands, shrub lands and deserts.

The echidna digs.

Spines protect its back.

The echidna has a soft belly.

It is protected by the ground.

Do echidnas dig quickly or slowly?

Draw What You See

How do we know what the continents look like?

People explore
unknown lands.

*Going to unknown places by walking,
sailing, sledding or flying.*

People measure
the land.

*Measurements from a transit or
global positioning system.*

People take photographs
of the land.

*Photographs and
radar from airplanes,
space shuttles and
satellites.*

Are there still
unexplored places
on earth?

Question answered on page 62

Draw a detailed map of the continents.

(Look at page 49 for directions on creating fold lines.)

1.

2.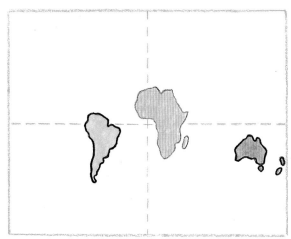

3.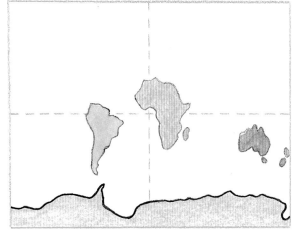

4.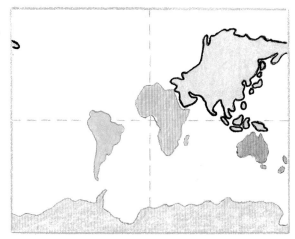

5.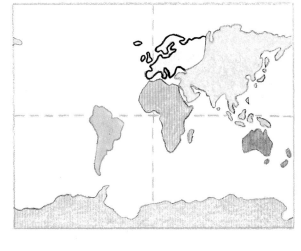

6.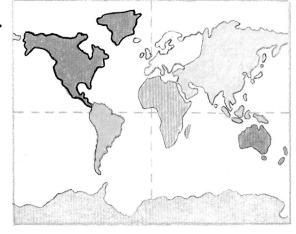

1. Label north and south on your map.

2. Label the Prime Meridian and the Equator.

3. Label the seven continents: Africa, South America, Australia, Antarctica, Asia, Europe and North America.

Learn more about Australian forest animals...

How far can a kangaroo jump?
Page 52

A large adult kangaroo can jump 25 feet — about the length of a bus! Australia has more than 70 kinds of kangaroos. There are very small kangaroos that live in trees and very large kangaroos that live in grasslands. Meet the kangaroos who live in the forests of Australia's east coast, called the gray kangaroo or "forester", in KANGAROO ISLAND *by Deirdre Langeland, illustrated by Frank Ordaz, published by Soundprints, 1998. See how an adventurous young kangaroo, a platypus, an echidna and a hopping mouse deal with a hungry crocodile in* SNAP! *by Marcia Vaughan, illustrated by Sascha Hutchinson, published by Scholastic, 1994.*

Do platypuses quack?
Page 55

No, platypuses do not quack. Follow the activities and growth of a young platypus with THE PLATYPUS *written by Pauline Reilly, illustrated by Will Rolland, published by Kangaroo Press, 1991.*

Are koalas safe when they go for a drink of water?
Page 56

Koalas don't leave the safety of the gum (eucalyptus) trees to drink water. Koalas get water from the moisture in the tree leaves! See koalas reach, eat, snuggle and snooze in MY FIRST PICTURE BOOK OF KOALAS *photographed by Steve Parish, published by Steve Parish Publishing, 1998.*

Do echidnas dig quickly or slowly?
Page 59

Echidnas dig quickly and efficiently when threatened. They appear to sink into the ground! The animal digs with all four legs, keeping its spines upright and its soft, unprotected belly against the soil. Follow the daily routine of a young echidna and experience the dangers it encounters with THE ECHIDNA *written by Pauline Reilly, illustrated by Will Rolland, published by Kangaroo Press, 1995.*

Learn more about mapmaking...

Which is easier to put in your pocket, a globe or a flat map?
Page 26

A flat map is almost always easier to put in a pocket. Understand how a flat map can represent our round world with ME ON THE MAP *by Joan Sweeney, illustrated by Annette Cable, published by Crown Publishers, 1996. An atlas is a book with a collection of flat maps. A good atlas to have on hand is* NATIONAL GEOGRAPHIC BEGINNER'S WORLD ATLAS *by National Geographic Society, 1999.*

Why is Greenland part of North America?
Page 48

Greenland is a large island located close to North America. Greenland, as drawn on the flat maps on page 48, appears much larger than it really is. Look at a globe for a more accurate scale model of the world, and become aware of map distortions with MAPS AND GLOBES *written by Jack Knowlton, illustrated by Harriett Barton, published by HarperTrophy, 1985. Then visit each continent with the curious space-traveling robots in* BLAST OFF TO EARTH! *written and illustrated by Loreen Leedy, published by Holiday House, 1992.*

Are there still unexplored places on earth?
Page 60

All the large areas of land on Earth are known and identified as continents, but areas within the continents are still being explored, like ravines in the tropical forests of Australia, ice shelves along Antarctica and the canopies of the South American rainforests. Follow the history of cartography and see how our knowledge of the earth continues to build in MAPPING A CHANGING WORLD *by Yvette La Pierre, published by Lickle, 1996. For a look at our world from space, see recent satellite photographs in* NATIONAL GEOGRAPHIC SATELLITE ATLAS OF THE WORLD *by National Geographic Society, 1998.*

Teaching Tips

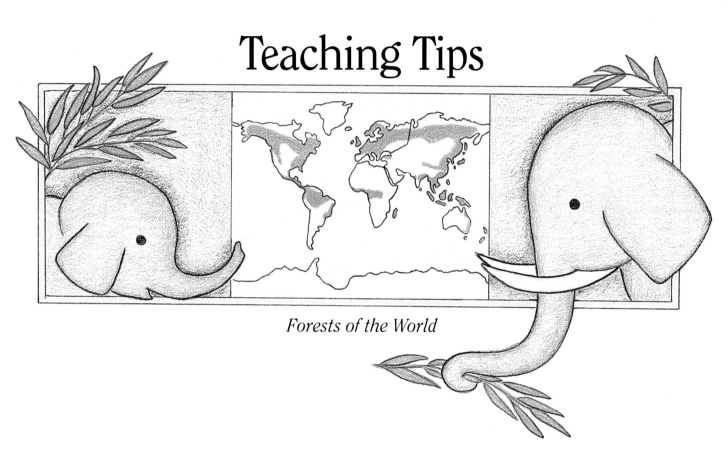

Forests of the World

Forest Animals of the Tropics

TIGER • BENGAL TIGER (page 12) — Sometimes artists omit lines when drawing in order to present a clearer picture. This lesson omits part of the line that defines the tiger's chin so we can get a good view of its whiskers and chin fur. The children erase much of the chin (step 4), then draw small curved lines for fur (step 4) and straight lines for whiskers (step 5). Would you like to draw a tiger lying down? Modify and combine this tiger lesson with the leopard lesson (page 16). Please note: Tigers do not climb trees!

LEOPARD (page 16) — Except for the spots and stripes, this lesson is similar to the tiger lesson. Read the tip for the tiger lesson (above).

MONKEY • SPIDER MONKEY (page 19) — Draw one monkey with the children, then challenge them to draw a second monkey hanging by its tail, running on a branch or reaching for fruit.

SLOTH • TWO-TOED SLOTH (page 24) — The sloth spends most of its life hanging from branches, so its fur grows toward its back. Compare the sloth's stiff, coarse fur to an animal with soft, flowing fur. Then demonstrate how straight coloring strokes, along with short, curved lines along the outline of the animal's body, can convey the texture of coarse fur.
Note: Sloths move so slowly that moss grows on their fur!

Sloth Fur

Skunk Fur

Animals of the Northern Forests

RED FOX (page 36) — This is another example of an artist omitting a line to present a clearer picture. (See the tiger lesson teaching tip). This drawing of a fox clearly shows the whiskers and nose with the white nose fur below the whiskers. It's chin is "hidden" behind the fur.

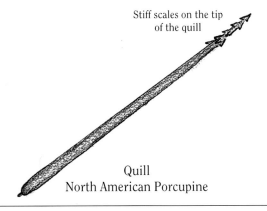

Stiff scales on the tip of the quill

Quill
North American Porcupine

PORCUPINE • NORTH AMERICAN PORCUPINE (page 40) — Draw the porcupine's body (steps 1 through 4) lightly with pencil. Use a crayon, marker or pencil to draw the quills (steps 5 through 8).

OPOSSUM • VIRGINIA OPOSSUM (page 44) — Opossums may have up to 13 babies in a litter! How many babies will the mother opossum have in your drawing?

Forest Animals Down Under

KOALA (page 56) — Koalas' front paws have two thumbs and three fingers (step 5). The back paws have one thumb and three fingers.

ECHIDNA (page 58) — The echidna drawings look adorable with 20 spines or 120 spines! Adjust the lesson to the children's ability and level of patience.

Pronunciation: ih-KID-nuh

Spines are solid. Quills are hollow.